STENCIL
SOURCE BOOK

Lucinda Ganderton

STENCIL
SOURCE BOOK

A Collection of 200 Stencil Designs

David & Charles

DEDICATION

For my son, Alexander

A DAVID & CHARLES BOOK

First published in the UK in 2001

Reprinted in 2001

Text copyright © Lucinda Ganderton 2001
Photography and layout Copyright © David & Charles 2001

A catalogue record for this book is available from the British Library.

ISBN 0 7153 1166 2

Commissioning editor	Lindsay Porter
Art editor	Ali Myer
Desk editor	Jennifer Proverbs
Photographer	Jon Bouchier

Printed in China by Leefung-Asco
for David & Charles
Brunel House, Newton Abbot, Devon

The images on pages 6–9 were supplied by David George/Elizabeth Whiting Associates.

Contents

 Country Style   24

Hearts, Butterflies, Cornucopia, Birds in Flight, Song Bird, Farmyard Birds, Arts and Crafts Animals, Farmyard Animals, Heraldic Unicorns, Reindeer, Noah's Ark, Lithuanian Folk Art, Spongeware Pottery, Russian Textiles, Scandinavian Embroidery, American Wall Stencils, Appliqué Designs, Patchwork Designs, Polish Flowers

 Classic Designs   58

Laurel Wreath, Palmate Border, Greek Key Border, Greek Urns, Roman Mosaic Border, Mosaic Bird, Fleur-de-lys, Lion and Eagle, Victorian Gothic, Italian Renaissance, Interlaced Diamond, Renaissance Brocades, Lily, Iris and Peony, Paisleys, Indian Elephant, Chinese Calligraphy, Ming Vase, Japanese Blossoms and Leaves, Round Celtic Knot, Book of Kells, Spanish Tile and Border, Art Nouveau Flowers, Mediterranean Sun and Stars, Alphabet and Numbers

 Flowers and Fruit   94

Parisian Fuchsia and Roses, Floral Sprigs, Nursery Flowers, Tulip and Carnation, Ottoman Carnation, Dutch Tulips and Vase, Roses and Ribbons, Primrose and Violets, Clematis, Bluebells, Daffodils, Sunflower, Basic Daisies, Chrysanthemum Border, Winter Berries Border, Cherry Blossom and Cherries, Apples and Pears, Autumn Leaves, Grapevine Border, Strawberries, Pineapple, Oranges and Lemons, Orange Tree, Peach Tree

 Marine and
Nautical Designs   128

Seaside Motifs, Skies, Lighthouse, Signalling Flags, Chain and wave borders, Knotted Rope Corner, Rope Borders, Anchors, Sailing Boats, Ship in a Bottle, Nursery Boats, Goldfish and Seaweed, Tropical Fish and Coral, Palm Trees, Dolphins, Sea Creatures, Seahorses, Starfish, Crab, Spiral Shells, Scallop and Pebbles

Introduction

Stencilling is one of the oldest methods of reproducing patterns and lettering directly onto a range of surfaces, from walls and floors to furniture and notices. It was used for fabric printing before the invention of silk screening and for colouring in wood-block illustrations. Despite its long history, the very simplicity and versatility of the technique means that it is still one of the most popular and widely practised paint effects for crafts and home decoration.

The term derives from the Middle English word 'stansel' which meant literally 'to ornament with various colours', and in Mediaeval times stencilled patterns were used to create rich, jewel-bright decoration for domestic and church interiors.

In the nineteenth century these were adapted by the Victorians as part of the Gothic

revival, and recent restoration work at the vast Midland Hotel in Central London has revealed polychromatic stencilling of dazzling complexity along corridors, staircases and in the cavernous reception rooms.

In the United States stencilling flourished from the 1770s to the 1860s in New England and Pennsylvania,

Gothic motifs and a simple triangular border in primary colours were used to stencil the cut-out bannisters of this wooden staircase.

A simple floral motif has been arranged in a half-drop repeat in this Scandinavian workroom.

influenced by the folk-art heritage of Dutch, German and Swiss immigrants. Indoors, stencils adorned chairs, tables, doors, window frames and tinware while outside wooden barns were stencilled with bold geometric symbols. More muted colours – a Gustavian palette of grey-greens and dusky creams and blues – were used in Scandinavian countries, where traditional stencilled and painted interiors have never lost their popularity.

The first commercial stencil designs were published over a hundred years ago and were immediately sought after by professionals and home enthusiasts alike. A practical guide from the 1920s, when the sun-ray shapes and formal patterns of art deco were ideally suited to stencilling, assured its readers that 'this work may be done by anyone [without artistic training] who has an eye for colour, and a little ingenuity in arranging patterns to produce a design'. At the same time Vanessa Bell and Duncan Grant were decorating the walls of their house at Charleston with spontaneous and lively geometric stencils.

Stencilling also has its more mundane uses. Thin sheets of metal pierced with lettering and trademarks, which now have a charm of their own, were used to label wooden packing cases containing goods ranging from the Shakers' garden seeds or crates of salted fish to lemons from the Italian port of Sorrento. Smaller stencils were also used to mark monograms onto laundry and stencilled notices can still be seen in various locations.

The contrasting effects of dark-on-light and light-on-dark stencilling have been combined to create a wallpaper-like effect of calm blues and greys.

Like the manual of the 1920s, this book is intended to provide an inspirational resource and image bank for everybody who is interested in stencilling, from beginners to the experienced designer. Whether you wish to make your own greetings cards or would enjoy the challenge of stencilling your bedroom in imitation of early American wall decoration, you are certain to find something that appeals.

There are over two hundred exciting new designs, grouped under four headings: Country Style, Classic Designs, Flowers and Fruit, and Marine and Nautical Designs. Each chapter includes a selection of large and small stencils, along with a choice of borders. These can all be used singly or as repeats, but some are designed to work together and can be built up to create a themed frieze or panel, such as the country-style Noah's Ark.

Getting started will not require a great initial outlay on special materials, as only a few basic tools and items of art equipment are required. New innovations — acetate sheeting, photocopying and heat pens — have greatly speeded up the process of making and adapting stencils, although manilla card is still the best medium for some designs. The next chapter shows you the basic techniques you will need to create your own stencils. Take time to experiment and develop your ideas by using different types of paint and unusual colour schemes, or by varying the scale of the design. You may choose to work in solid blocks of pure colour for a contemporary look or prefer a softer, more antique style in combination with colour washing and other paint effects. Whatever you produce, it will be your own personal vision: no two individuals will ever interpret a stencil in the same way.

Border designs can be worked vertically as well as horizontally, and look particularly effective when other motifs are added.

Essential Techniques

Basic stencilling techniques are very simple: the key to

successful results is to ensure the paint is not applied so

thickly that it drips or seeps underneath the stencil itself.

Once you are familiar with the basic methods for applying

colour, you can develop your technique to create different

paint effects and patterns. The instructions on the following

pages will explain how to create your own stencils from

the motifs in this book, and how to use the stencils for

a variety of effects.

Materials and equipment

Stencilling does not require a great deal of specialist equipment, although there are some items on the market that may make the technique easier. If you plan to use your stencil design over and over again, for example, you will need to ensure it is made from a durable material such as acetate.

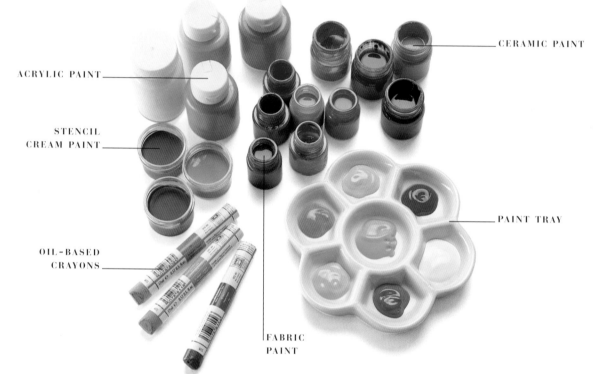

ACRYLIC PAINT

CERAMIC PAINT

STENCIL CREAM PAINT

OIL-BASED CRAYONS

PAINT TRAY

FABRIC PAINT

WATER-BASED PAINTS

Water-based ACRYLIC PAINT, in tubes and pots, can be used directly or mixed to produce your own shades. The thick creamy paint is quick drying and, when applied thinly, will not seep below the stencil. TEXTURE GELS, which consist of minute plastic granules in a clear medium, can be mixed with acrylics. Several manufacturers produce ranges of STENCIL PAINTS in country-style or traditional colours, while EMULSION SAMPLE POTS are a good source of unusual colours for walls.

OIL-BASED PAINTS

These solid paints take longer to dry but the colours blend well and give a rich, smooth finish. They are available in stick form as STENCIL CRAYONS or as STENCIL CREAM PAINT in flat screw-top pots. METALLIC WAX comes in a range of colours from aluminium to bronze and is ideal for highlighting areas within a design.

CERAMIC PAINTS

These brightly coloured paints, available in opaque and translucent versions, can be fired in a domestic oven and can be used to decorate pottery or glass.

FABRIC PAINTS

Specially designed for working on textiles, these water-based paints can be fixed with the heat of an iron and washed gently by hand.

A PAINT TRAY is useful for mixing colours, but an old saucer or spare tile can also be used as a palette.

VARNISH

Spray matt or gloss varnish will protect your finished stencils, and should always be used on walls, furniture or others areas that will undergo a lot of wear and tear.

STENCIL BRUSHES

The heads of these brushes are made from stiff, densely packed bristles, specially designed for applying paint with a stippling action. They are available in sizes from 5mm to 4cm (¼in to 1¾in) – use the smallest for adding detail and for intricate designs and the largest for quick coverage. NATURAL SPONGES are the best tool for painting large, textured areas.

TOOLS FOR MAKING STENCILS

A selection of hard and soft PENCILS and a fine pen are used with TRACING PAPER AND/OR CARBON PAPER for transferring designs onto STENCIL CARD. This is a pliable manilla board impregnated with linseed oil to make it waterproof. A sharp CRAFT KNIFE with a fine blade or a SCALPEL is used to cut out the stencil shapes, and a METAL RULER is essential for accurate straight lines within a design. For safety you should always work onto a CUTTING MAT.

Transparent or semi-opaque ACETATE STENCIL FILM is easy to cut with a craft knife, but if you intend to make a lot of stencils it is worth investing in a HEAT KNIFE which melts through the acetate. You will need a sheet of GLASS to use as a working surface.

FIXING THE STENCIL

STENCIL ADHESIVE is a re-positionable spray which is used to hold card or acetate stencils flat against the surface being painted. Strips of LOW-TACK MASKING TAPE will secure the edges of the stencil without damaging the background.

How to make a card stencil

Oiled manilla card is the traditional medium for making strong, durable stencils, particularly for larger scale designs, geometric patterns or those based on straight lines or smooth curves. The design is first traced onto the card, then cut out with a sharp knife. The finished stencil can be varnished before use to make it more durable.

1 TRACING FROM A BOOK
Fix a piece of tracing paper over the page with low-tack tape, then draw round each element within the stencil using a sharp, hard pencil. Place the paper face down and rub over the reverse of the outlines with a soft pencil. Turn the paper over and tape it to the card, leaving a margin of at least 2cm (¾in) all round. To transfer the image, carefully draw over the outlines once again using the hard pencil or a ball-point pen.

2 TRACING FROM A PHOTOCOPY
To change the size of your chosen stencil, enlarge or reduce the design on a photocopier. Cut a piece of card approximately 5cm (2in) larger than the image. Place a sheet of carbon paper face down onto the card, then fix the photocopy over it with low-tack masking tape. Draw around each individual stencil shape using a ball-point pen. Peel off the photocopy and carbon and fill in any parts of the outline that may have been missed.

3 CUTTING OUT WITH A CRAFT KNIFE
Secure the card onto a cutting mat both for safety and to avoid the blade becoming blunt. Using a sharp scalpel or craft knife, cut accurately around each outline, without applying too much pressure. Keep the knife upright and cut towards you, rotating the board as necessary when working around complicated shapes. Remember that patience and a steady hand are essential. Any mistakes can be repaired with a small patches of ordinary masking tape on each side of the stencil.

How to make an acetate stencil

Transparent acetate may not be as durable as stencil card but it has many advantages. The design does not have to be transferred and it is easy to cut, making it ideal for smaller-scale designs. Using a heat knife not only speeds up the process, but enables you to cut out the most intricate curves and spirals quickly and easily.

1 SECURING THE ACETATE
Place a sheet of glass over the chosen page if you are working directly from the book or over a photocopy if you wish to enlarge or reduce the stencil. Cut a piece of acetate slightly larger than the design, spray the back very lightly with re-positioning adhesive and fix centrally to the glass with low-tack masking tape, making sure that none of the image is concealed.

2 CUTTING OUT WITH A HEAT PEN
The stencil can now be cut out with a knife, following the same rules as for stencil card (see opposite). If you prefer to use a heat pen, study the manufacturer's instructions carefully and take time to practise on an offcut before starting. Run the point of the pen smoothly and steadily around each outline, ensuring that you do not to leave it on one spot for too long or a small hole will appear.

3 FINISHING OFF THE STENCIL
Remove the tape and gently peel the stencil away from the glass. The heat pen will have melted through the acetate: ease out any shapes that have not fallen away and trim any rough edges with a pair of small sharp scissors.

How to stencil

Make sure the surface you are going to work on is clean and primed if necessary, then decide where the stencil is to go. Spray the reverse of the stencil with re-positioning adhesive and smooth it gently in place. Tape the edges down with low-tack masking tape for extra security and to prevent the paint going over the stencil.

Stencilling with acrylics

1 **APPLYING THE FIRST COLOUR**
Pour a small amount of water-based paint onto a saucer. Load the tip of the brush with paint, then rub off the surplus onto a scrap of paper so that it is distributed evenly between the bristles. Working from the sides of each space inwards, apply the colour through the stencil using a stippling action and keeping the brush upright. Use an offcut of paper to mask off the areas which will be another colour.

2 **APPLYING THE SECOND COLOUR**
To keep the colours from becoming muddy, use a separate brush for each colour, or wash the first brush with mild detergent and dry with a hair dryer. Load and then prime the bristles as before and apply the paint sparingly, building up several fine layers of colour rather than one thick one.

3 **ADDING SHADING**
Applying a darker colour to the edges of the stencil will create a three-dimensional effect. Wait until the paint is completely dry before peeling off the tape and removing the stencil. To keep the outlines sharp, wipe off any excess paint and clean the stencil with kitchen paper before using it again. Store your stencils in a shallow drawer or stiff envelope to keep them flat.

How to make a two-layered stencil

1 USING STENCIL CARD
Cut out two pieces of stencil card, each at least 4cm (1½in) larger all round than the stencil. Transfer the main outline onto the first piece following the instructions on page 14, making sure that you include the four registration marks. Rule four lines across the stencil to link the crosses, then cut out the corners.

2 REGISTRATION MARKS
Make the second stencil in the same way, transferring only the detailed areas in the darker colour. Tape down the first stencil, marking a small L-shape in pencil at each corner. Fill the stencil in using a single, solid colour, then remove the card when the paint is dry. Line the second stencil up so that the corners match the L-shapes, then tape it down and add the second colour.

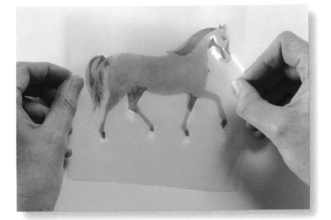

3 USING ACETATE
Two-layered stencils cut from transparent acetate are much simpler to use than card as they can be lined up by eye. Coat the back of the second stencil lightly with adhesive and match it up to the main outline, using the image in the book as a guide.

Applying colour

Oil-based crayons

These crayons are made from solid pigment: some colour ranges are specially manufactured for stencilling but you can also use artists' oil sticks. They are easier to work with than water-based acrylics as there is no risk of overloading the brush, but they do take longer – up to two days – to dry completely. Varnish the completed design to protect it from wear and tear.

1 LOADING THE BRUSH
Rub the tip of the crayon onto an offcut of card to break the hard surface, then draw a small circle of pigment. Load the brush by swirling the bristles in the softened paint, ensuring that they are evenly coated.

2 APPLYING THE COLOUR
Keeping the brush upright, apply the paint through the stencil using a gentle swirling action to create a smooth surface. This technique produces solid blocks of colour, but the addition of extra shades gives a smooth, blended finish to the shapes.

Fabric Paints

Stencils work well on fabrics and can be used to decorate a variety of soft furnishings and clothing. Use special fabric paints which can be laundered by hand and prepare the cloth by washing it to remove any dressings and pressing well. Plain cottons are easy to use, but experiment with metallic paints on velvet or organza for a more luxurious effect.

1 APPLYING THE PAINT
Protect the back of the fabric with a pad of paper towels to prevent the paint seeping through. Apply the colour sparingly and work it well into the fabric with the bristles to achieve an even effect. Allow to dry completely, then fix the paint with an iron, according to the manufacturer's instructions.

Sponging

Sponging is the quickest technique for covering larger areas. It produces an interesting mottled effect which can be embellished careful with shading. Use a natural sponge for an open, grainy finish or a synthetic kitchen sponge for a finer look. Fast-drying acrylic paints are ideal for sponging and should be slightly diluted before use.

1 PREPARING THE SPONGE
If you are using a natural sponge, soften it before you start by rinsing in warm water and wringing out the moisture. Depending on the size of the stencil, dab part or all of the sponge onto a palette of diluted paint, then work off the excess on a paper towel until the sponge itself is almost dry.

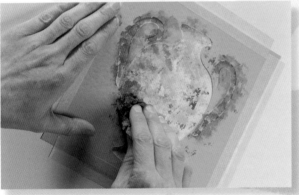

2 APPLYING THE COLOUR
Apply the paint through the stencil by repeatedly dabbing it over the surface, building up a soft, textured finish. To create the three-dimensional effect on this urn motif, the palest colour was used first, then layers of progressively darker paint were built up around the edges of the shape.

Using aerosol paint

Aerosol paint is also used for fast results and for large, bold stencils. The fine mist of paint produced by the spray carries easily, so mask off an area of at least 30cm (12in) around your stencil with newsprint or tracing paper to prevent the colour spreading. If you are working in a confined area it is a sensible precaution to wear a protective mask.

1 SPRAYING THE SURFACE
Fix the stencil in place as usual and protect the surrounding area. Hold the can about 20cm (8in) from the stencil and spray the paint across it in smooth layers for even coverage. Keep your hand moving to prevent the colour building up in one place and running, and allow each fine layer to dry before adding the next.

Paint finishes

Stencilling is an incredibly versatile medium. There is a huge variety of effects that can be created and no two people will use a stencil in the same way. You may want to reproduce an antique, faded design with soft stippling, create a contemporary image in patches of intense colour, or print your own curtain fabric. With a little imagination and experimentation you will find that by changing the size of the image and colours and types of paint that you use, you can produce your own very individual interpretations.

STIPPLING
Great depth can be added to a stencil worked in just one colour by building up areas of denser paint within the design.

SHADED STIPPLING
Paint the lightest colours in first, then add darker shades to the edges of the stencils to create a three-dimensional effect.

SWIRLED SHADING
For a more solid effect with a smooth surface, use a swirling action to apply the paint. Follow the direction of the shapes to imitate brushstrokes.

TEXTURE GEL

Acrylic gels add visual interest to the surface of the stencilled design: here a sand-like texture has been used to create a real seaside effect.

FABRIC PAINTS

You can stencil onto ready-made garments such as t-shirts, or onto a length of plain fabric which can be made up as you wish.

SPONGING

Sponging with poster paints would be a good introduction to stencilling for children, but this quick technique gives sophisticated results.

METALLIC WAX

This lustrous specialist paint should be applied with a soft cloth and allowed to dry completely before the stencil is removed.

SPRAY PAINT

Aerosol paint gives a slightly speckled texture to the finished stencil – you can add more depth by over-painting in a darker colour.

CERAMIC PAINT

Ceramic paints can be applied in thin layers with a sponge or – as here – built up thickly with a brush to produce a solid effect.

Composing your design

Stencils can be used singly to decorate small items, but when covering a large surface such as a wall, floor or wooden chest, you will need to use the design several times or combine two or more stencils to make a composite image. This creates a whole realm of design potential and allows you to explore the many different ways in which one motif can create an all-over pattern.

Running border

A stencilled border can be used within a room at dado or cornice level to break up large expanses of plain wall. To mark the position of the border, draw a series of points, approximately 30cm (12in) apart, which will line up with the bottom edge of the stencil. Join them with pencil, then check this base line is straight with a spirit level. Start at the left end of the border.

1 TRANSFERRING REGISTRATION MARKS
Transfer the registration marks onto the stencil to ensure that the repeats line up correctly. Cut two small notches on the top and bottom edges in line with the crosses. Spray the stencil with adhesive, line up the bottom edge with the base line and lightly mark the two right-hand notches on the wall with pencil before taping down.

2 LINING UP THE STENCIL
Match up the stencil for the second and subsequent repeats by lining up the two left-hand notches with the previous pencil marks. Always mark in the right-hand notches before attaching the stencil. The pencil lines can be removed with a soft eraser.

Creating mirror images

By simply reversing a stencil you can create a lively and dynamic effect. Draw a horizontal base line and line up the first image at the left-hand side. Clean any surplus paint from the stencil card, leave to dry, then turn it over. Leaving a small space, line up the bottom of the stencil with the base line and paint the second repeat.

Creating a half-drop repeat

If you have sufficient patience, this technique can be used to cover an entire wall in imitation of wallpaper. To achieve a professional result, use a plumb line to make sure that the first stencil is positioned vertically, and keep checking with a spirit level as you progress.

1 MARKING UP THE STENCIL
Cut an accurate rectangle of stencil card and divide it into quarters. Snip a small triangular notch at the end of each line. Transfer the design centrally and cut it out. Fix the stencil in the first position at the left of the wall. Lightly draw a small cross at the centre of the notches and at each corner, then tape down and paint.

2 POSITIONING THE THIRD STENCIL
For the second repeat, line up the left side of the stencil with the marks on the right of the first image. Match the bottom corner and centre notch to the top two crosses and fill in the other crosses before taping the stencil down and painting. Line up the top left corner with the crosses as shown for the third repeat, then continue working across and downwards to fill the required space.

Repeating around a centre point

Use this method with square stencils to create an all-over pattern. Cut an accurate square of card or acetate 3cm (1¼in) larger than the design and draw a diagonal line linking two opposite corners. Transfer the design so it is in line with this mark and equidistant from the sides of the square. Draw two base lines at right angles. Match the inner edges of the stencil to one corner and paint the first repeat. Turn the stencil by 45 degrees before painting in the second repeat, then work the remaining stencils in the same way.

Country Style

Folk artists from around the world have always looked to their natural surroundings for inspiration. The stencils in this chapter include designs from as far afield as North America, Eastern Europe and Scandinavia. They reflect this wealth of tradition and feature a varied range of trees, birds, animals, stylized fruit and flowers, as well as patterns derived from country crafts such as appliqué, patchwork, embroidery and painted furniture.

Hearts

Heart motifs, which traditionally symbolize love and affection, are found in the folk art of many countries. These derive from Pennsylvania Dutch designs of the nineteenth century.

Butterflies

These butterflies would work well with any of the larger flower designs from Flowers and Fruit. The colour of the silhouettes can be adapted to fit any colour scheme.

Cornucopia

The cornucopia, or horn of plenty, represents fertility and bounty and has been used as a design motif since classical times. This version is based on the extravagant American appliqué quilts produced in Baltimore in the 1860s.

Birds in Flight

Inspired by an Arts and Crafts woodcut from the early twentieth century, these flying birds can be used singly or as a border with the song bird.

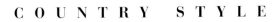
Song Bird

This motif was adapted from early
American appliqué – a 'Bird of
Paradise' quilt made for a bride from
New York state in 1860.

Farmyard Birds

The strong outline of this farmyard cockerel comes from an antique copper weathervane. The original had a rich verdigris patina, so more naturalistic colours have been added to the stencil design. The geese opposite can be worked in similar tones.

Arts and Crafts Animals

In the early twentieth century, the influences of Art Nouveau were combined with the folk-art traditions revived by William Morris and his followers – as shown in these stylized bird and hare designs.

Farmyard Animals

The details on the larger horse and the dog are added to the basic outline with a second stencil (see page 17): alternatively the darker areas can be painted in by hand with a fine paintbrush.

Heraldic Unicorns

Reindeer

These two reindeer – one leaping and one walking – would make ideal Christmas card designs, or they could accompany the other animals into the Ark (see next page).

Noah's Ark

The Ark was a favourite country-style theme and featured in paintings as well as the familiar carved toy. This version, which can be used to make a nursery frieze, comes complete with a dove of peace. Stencil two of each animal to make the pairs, varying the colours slightly to distinguish them and adding the markings with a smaller brush. There are separate stencils for the cow and bull.

Noah's Ark

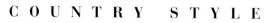
Lithuanian Folk Art

This red and green ivy wreath is an ideal Christmas design. Like the bird tree opposite, which is based on traditional painted window shutters, it comes from Eastern Europe.

Spongeware Pottery

Simple motifs like these flowers, hearts and leaves were as popular with potters in the nineteenth century as they are today. They were cut from potatoes or dense foam, dipped in liquid glaze and used to stamp borders and patterns on country-style ceramics – plates, mugs, basins and jugs.

Russian Textiles

This delicate willow tree is based on a printed cotton design from St Petersburg. The hearts derive from a heavily embroidered shawl design and can be used singly or in rows as a border.

Scandinavian Embroidery

The Scandinavian countries have a rich heritage of decorative arts, especially embroidery. These three motifs come from a Finnish sampler, worked in cross stitch. Make a tiny extra stencil for the cockerel's heart, or add it by hand.

American Wall Stencils

*Patterned wallpapers were fashionable in
the late eighteenth century, but prohibitively
expensive, so stencilling proved the ideal
substitute. Itinerant decorators specialized in
working directly onto plain plastered walls.
These nosegay and border motifs reflect the
charming simplicity of their designs.*

Appliqué Designs

*Flowers and hearts are an enduring
and popular combination. These
designs, inspired by appliqué, could
be stencilled onto fabric and quilted
in imitation of the originals.*

Patchwork Designs

This patchwork pattern, known as 'Sunburst' is worked in warm oranges and golds. When the same design is used in shades of blue it is known as 'Mariner's Compass', and could be used with the nautical stencils in Chapter 4. The 'Basket of Grapes' and 'Eight Point Star' opposite are based on simple arrangements of squares and triangles.

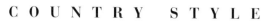
Polish Flowers

The subtly shaded tulip urn opposite is
a reworking of a traditional papercut
design while the rose basket and
floral spray motif are based
on a brightly coloured
stencilled dish.

Classic Designs

Classic and historic patterns have long provided a rich source

of inspiration for artists and architects, and each new

generation has re-interpreted designs from the past in a new

and contemporary style. The stencils on the following pages

span 2,000 years of decorative art and design across the

globe, from ancient Roman mosaics and Chinese ceramics

to illuminated Celtic manuscripts, Mediaeval tiles and

twentieth-century art movements.

Laurel Wreath

A garland of evergreen laurel leaves is an ancient symbol of victory and peace – as well as being a classic decorative motif.

Palmate Border

This design is based on a border from ancient Greece. Start stencilling this border by painting in all three design elements. Continue the repeat by lining up the registration mark on the lower edge and repeat the three-petalled flower and the palm to the end of the line. Paint a final 's' shape below and to the right of the final palm.

Greek Key Border

Begin at the left by working the whole stencil. To continue, block off the first half of the motif with masking tape, then match the registration marks and work towards the right. Work the left half of the motif only to fill in the space at the end of the border.

Greek Urns

Sponging (see page 19) is a quick and direct stencilling method which gives a frescoed effect to these urns.

Roman Mosaic Border

This trompe-l'oeil twisted border is a recurring motif in Roman mosaic floor patterns where it was used as an edging and to separate decorative panels within the design.

Mosaic Bird

This dove can be used as a single motif, in pairs with one reversed or in conjunction with the mosaic border on the opposite page.

Fleur-de-lys

The larger of these motifs is derived from the ceramic tiles used in English cathedrals in the Middle Ages. The fleur-de-lys can be used upright as a spot motif or repeated around a centre point to create a square pattern (see page 23).

Lion and Eagle

Heraldic creatures like these were used in the Middle Ages to decorate ceilings and walls, as well as painted furniture and embroidered banners.

Victorian Gothic

During the Victorian era there was a great revival of interest in the art of the Mediaeval period. Encaustic floor tiles with formal *patterns like these were mass-produced for domestic use and widely used in hallways and garden paths. Large scale stencils, like that opposite, were used to decorate walls and furniture.*

Italian Renaissance

These three floral designs are derived from the lavishly patterned fabrics used for clothing and furnishings during the fourteenth and fifteenth centuries, and which feature in paintings from that period.

Interlaced Diamond

Fretwork patterns like this interlaced motif were used on a small scale in black and white to ornament the pages of early printed books.

Renaissance Brocades

Symmetrical motifs like these are characteristic of brocade designs, originally woven in heavy silk. Repeated in a half-drop pattern (see page 23) they work well on a large expanse of wall or fabric.

Lily, Iris and Peony

These two flowers and the peony design opposite are based on greatly enlarged designs from eighteenth-century Indian miniature paintings, which are jewel-like and rich in colour and detail.

Paisleys

The paisley is one of the oldest decorative motifs in the applied arts. It became popular in Europe and America when woven and embroidered shawls were exported from India. Its modern name comes from the Scottish town where western versions were made.

Indian Elephant

*Like the lily and iris designs on page 74,
this trumpeting elephant is based on a
detail from a miniature painting.*

Chinese Calligraphy

PEACE, HARMONY

BALANCE

PROSPERING

COMPLETE

Ming Vase

Blue and white is a favourite colour scheme for Chinese ceramics, and one which inspired much work in other countries.

Japanese Blossoms and Leaves

This selection of motifs comes from Japanese lacquer work, embroidery, stencilled fabric and painting.

Round Celtic Knot

The never-ending line of this circular motif and the square knot opposite is a symbol of harmony and infinity which recurs throughout Celtic art.

Book of Kells

These small motifs are enlargements of the details which appear in the margins of the Book of Kells, one of the world's most significant and beautiful illuminated manuscripts.

Spanish Tile and Border

Like the fleur-de-lys, this square stencil can be used as an upright diamond, or repeated in blocks of four around a centre point (see page 23) to create an all-over design. It works well with the textured green border opposite.

Art Nouveau Flowers

Stylized flowers, like these rosebud and tulip motifs and the rose border opposite, are typical of the elegant Art Nouveau style which flourished at the turn of the nineteenth century. Their sinuous lines adapt well to stencilling.

Mediterranean Sun and Stars

*The sun, surrounded by its rays, is a
motif which recurs in all cultures. This
version, along with the stars opposite, is
worked in the warm yellows and ochres
of the Mediterranean countries.*

abcd
efghij
klmn

opqrs

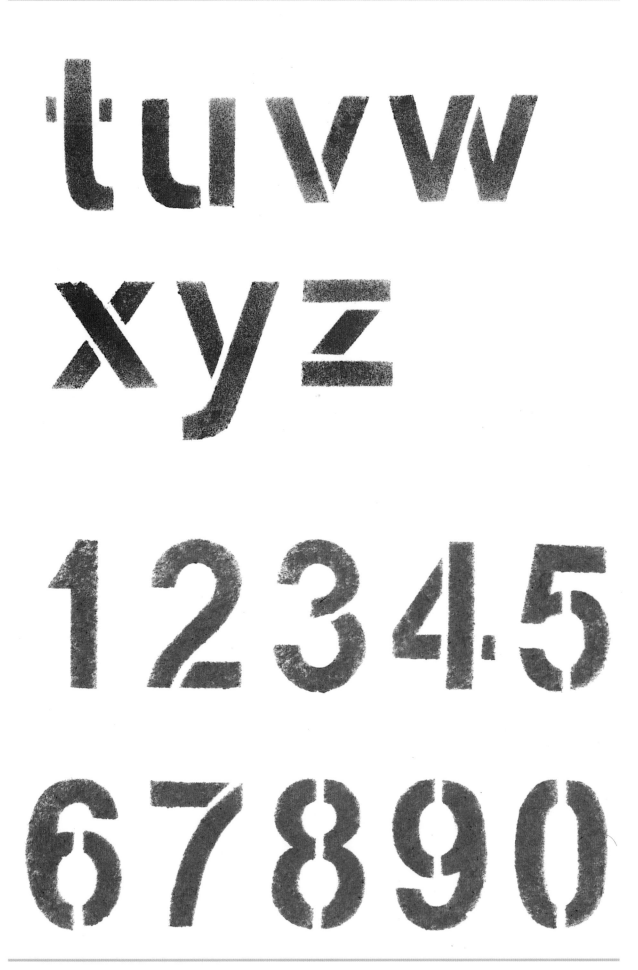

Flowers
and Fruit

The infinitely varied shapes and colours of flowers and fruits

are the inspiration behind the stencils in this chapter, which

range in style from naive daisies to sophisticated art-deco

ribbons and roses. The designs loosely follow the four seasons,

starting with the clear, bright colours of spring primroses,

daffodils and violets. These are followed by the full-blown

roses of high summer, the rich colours of the autumn harvest

and the frosted leaves and berries of winter.

Parisian Fuchsia and Roses

These spray motifs and checked border, reminiscent of French country pottery, can be worked in different colour schemes to vary the effect: see the examples on page 22 for ideas.

Floral Sprigs

Small-scale dress prints from the early nineteenth century have been greatly enlarged and re-coloured in bright contemporary shades to create these simple floral designs.

Nursery Flowers

These bold tulips and daisies in primary colours are perfect for children's rooms and can be used on walls, fabric or furniture.

Tulip and Carnation
These two motifs are inspired by the botanical woodcuts used to illustrate herbals, which in turn influenced many seventeenth-century embroidery designs.

Ottoman Carnation

This more formal design is typical of the textiles produced in the Middle East, where the carnation was cultivated for its delicate scent and colour.

Dutch Tulips and Vase

Blue and white Delft pottery, along with tulips, are synonymous with The Netherlands, where entire fortunes were gambled on a single bulb during the 'Tulipomania' speculation of the 1630s.

Roses and Ribbons

These feminine designs of dusky pink roses and pale turquoise ribbons have an Art Deco feel which is reminiscent of a glamorous 1930s boudoir.

Primrose and Violets

Clematis

The Clematis Montana flower is
stencilled in pale purple and the detail
on the petals and in the centre is added
using a fine brush and darker colours.

Bluebells

Daffodils

Sunflower

The shading which gives a three-dimensional effect for the flower centre is created by working concentric circles in different colours.

To make a tall sunflower, draw a green stalk directly onto the wall, stencil pairs of leaves at regular intervals and top it off with a flower head.

Simple Daisies

Chrysanthemum Border

Like the frosted berry design opposite, this naive leaf and flower pattern can be used singly or repeated to make a border.

Winter Berries Border

This Art Nouveau-style pattern could be worked in warmer tones to complement the rosebud, tulip and rose designs on pages 86 and 87.

Cherry Blossom and Cherries

Use the palest pinks and the richest reds for these stencils, along with delicate greens for the leaves and darker shades for the cherries.

Apples and Pears

The russet colours of the apple and subtle shades of the conference pears are built up in light layers to give a three-dimensional effect. The Victorian design opposite, based on a scrap, is coloured in the same way.

Autumn Leaves

Add to this group of stencils by collecting and pressing your own leaves. Draw around the outlines directly onto card and simplify the shapes if necessary as you cut them out.

Grapevine Border

Grapes and vine leaves – here worked in rich harvest tones – have been a favourite design motif since Roman times.

Strawberries

Paint the strawberries in flat colour and, using a fine brush, paint on a sprinkling of yellow dots afterwards to represent the seeds.

Pineapple

This extravagant fruit has long been a symbol of hospitality, and often features on gates and over doorways to welcome visitors to the house.

Oranges and Lemons

Use bright citrus shades to paint these simple fruit designs and build up the texture of peel with shaded layers of stippling.

Orange Tree

This intricate design works best when worked in blocks of plain colour, with the oranges picked out in stippling. The velvety texture of the fruit opposite is created by using a dry brush to stipple several layers of closely matched shades of pink and peach.

Peach Tree

Marine and Nautical Designs

Fish, shells and seahorses are perennial favourites for

decorating bathrooms, but this chapter illustrates a wider

selection of maritime designs. The seaside holiday stencils

include brightly coloured buckets, spades and beach huts,

while tropical coral, dolphins and palm trees add a more

exotic note. Sailing ships, fishing boats and steamers are

accompanied by flags, ropes, anchors and wave designs.

Seaside Motifs

Recreate those long sunny summer days on the beach with these favourite motifs of childhood. Use the brightest colours for the bucket, spade and ball (on page 132) and add texture to the sandcastle with sponging or a texture gel (see Paint finishes, page 21).

Seaside Motifs

Skies

These clouds and flocks of birds can be used to add a background to the seaside motifs or to the lighthouse, boats and ships on the following pages. Work the clouds in white against a blue background or in pale greys on white.

Lighthouse

The granite effect of the rocks is created by working light layers of grey and black paint with a very dry brush. Fade out the yellow paint along the beams of light to achieve a realistic effect.

Signalling Flags

Nautical flags have been used by sailors over the centuries to communicate with the shore and to send messages to other ships. Each letter of the alphabet is represented by its own flag.

A

D

B

E

C

F

Chain and Wave Borders

Knotted Rope Corner

This corner motif can be used in conjunction with the narrow rope border on page 138 to create a square or rectangular panel.

Rope Borders

These borders work well with any of the nautical motifs, especially the anchors opposite.

Anchors

Sailing Boats

Ship in a Bottle

The first layer – the bottle – of this stencil should be worked in pale stippled blues to give a translucent effect. Add flecks of white to the sea to create the effect of crashing waves.

Nursery Boats

The yacht and jaunty steamer on this page, along with the traditional Cornish fishing boat, could be combined to make a frieze or border for a child's bedroom. Repeat the wave motifs to create a deeper sea.

Goldfish and Seaweed

These fish could be worked in any colour to vary the effect. Paint in the eye details by hand, using a fine brush.

Tropical Fish and Coral

The exotic outlines of angel fish and other tropical species make ideal and interesting shapes for stencils. Choose clear, bright shades and work in flat patches of colour or create a more three-dimensional look with shading.

Palm Trees

Add the clouds and seagulls from page 133 to these palm trees to make your own desert island scene.

Dolphins

Sea Creatures

The swirling shapes of the octopus, jelly fish and sea anenomes can be used with the coral and sea horses to create an underwater world.

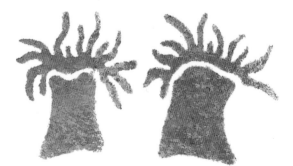

Seahorses

Starfish

The drop shadow which gives a solid effect to the two smaller starfish is easy to achieve. Work the stencil in a pale grey or beige shade and allow to dry. Re-position the stencil to the right of, and slightly above, the outline and paint in a darker colour.

Crab

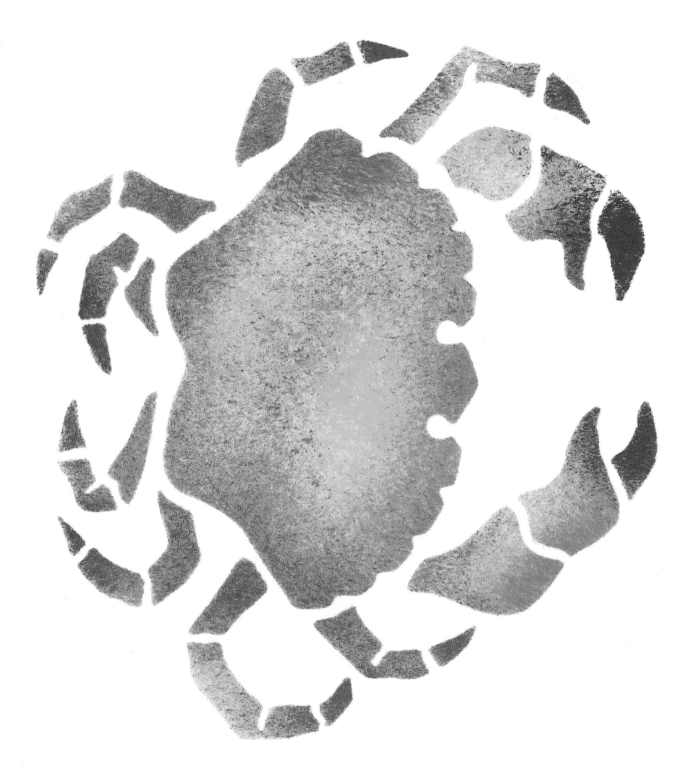

Spiral Shells

Choose the palest shades of lemon, pink and brown to give a realistic feel to these shells, or darker, brighter colours for a more dramatic look.

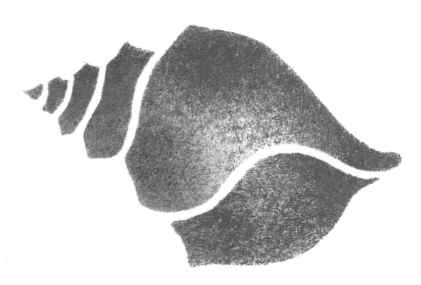

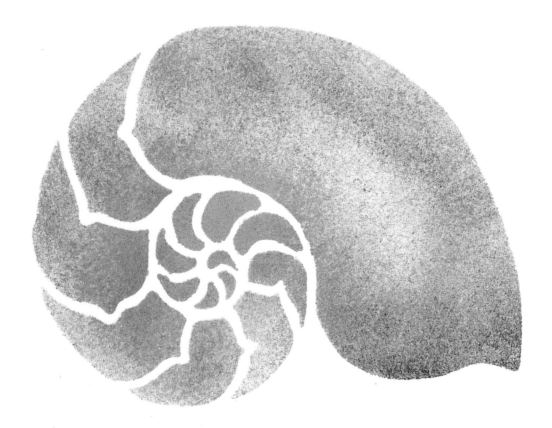

Scallop and Pebbles

The outline of the smooth pebbles is very simple – the three-dimensional effect is created by building up layers of paint. A similar shaded effect gives a solid feel to the scallop shell.

Simple Shells and Coral

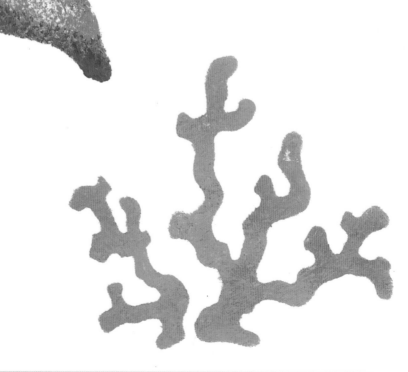

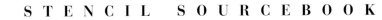
Index

Tools and techniques

Stencil subjects